Pain on Paper

By:

Arica Robinson

"I have learned to forgive the person I was and accepted the person I am to be the greatest person I can be."

Pain on Paper

Dedication

In loving memory of Rosa B. Broomfield, for seeing better for me than I could even imagine for myself. You Always knew the right words to say, and when I did not want to listen, your words stuck with me always.

Arica J. Robinson

Pain on Paper

Table of Contents

Pain on Paper

Pain on Paper

Introduction

I am on a journey of self-discovery, and I want to help young people discover who they are along the way. Instead of being hindered by our many different traumas and life experiences, we should learn to forgive our past, and grab hold of our future. I am a woman who knows silence very well. I know the smell of a person who has been so traumatized they are too afraid to open their mouths. I have been that person, who was afraid to speak or only spoke when spoken to. I want to share my story with you, show you that it is alright to be bold. You do not have to be silent about your story, you can be open and honest about who you are and what you have been through.

I am releasing my story out into the world, in hopes that you will make better decisions for yourself. I want people to know they are not alone, and there's power in being who you are. Unfortunately, we cannot always have it our way!

Pain on Paper

Realize it or not, our lives have all been planned out for us. I believe in purpose and that life has an expected ending. I believe we have life experience, whether good or bad, it is all for a specific reason. We all carry a purpose!

It is how we chose to deal with the life experiences that can shape and mold our future. The story of my life, my not so perfect life, is a breath of fresh air for me to say to you. To admit to myself and others that I am not perfect. And that is okay not to be. I wanted to be perfect, but only for the wrong reasons.

Life really did not go as planned. There is an order to life that was pressure on me at an early age: Go to grade school, to receive good grades, go to college to get a good paying job. Get married and have no babies before then. I am not saying it is a bad order, but it was an order that almost made it seem like there was no room for mistakes or slight detours, because all decisions are not mistakes. You are left to figure out the what ifs on your own! Most people do not teach you about the what ifs of life, they do not tell you that negative things will happen in your life and how you can move on successfully.

It may take you longer than others, whatever the case may be you can do it. Believe in yourself, no matter the past, just keep moving. Trust your process and put a smile
on your face because life is not done with us yet.

I hope you find yourself while reading my story. I hope it helps you to grow, and heal, so that you can move on to a happier, healthier life. We may have more in common with each other than you would think. For example, people watching! We all do it, and it can be quite entertaining at times. Every day you see people doing everyday things. Whether it be walking to the car, shopping, or reading a book at Starbucks. In most cases you would not second guess if that person were really okay or are, they at one with themselves and their many situations.

However, those same people who smiled at you

in passing and asked how you were doing at the cash register, are shattering inside. Those people are wondering the same thing you and I have been wondering. When will someone stand up for me, love me, protect me and always be there for me? How can I be there for that person in need? Where is our cure, or our happy ending? When will the pain and emotions stop? Hear this when I say, it will not stop! The truth is, if you stay stuck in that one place of unforgiveness, it will not stop!

Forgiveness. Forgive what? Forgive yourself for starters. Forgive you for not loving you, forgive you for not being your own happy ending, forgive you for not standing up! Forgive yourself for not making the right choices. We make such a big mess at just pointing the finger, when sometimes we need to just be free and say I forgive you, to whoever it may be. It may not be just you, you may have to forgive a friend, your mom, your dad or that stranger you would rather not see again. You can free yourself.

Pain on Paper

Forgiveness is the cure that so many people need to hear. There is no big secret about it, we just have to learn to be free to become free, to live in freedom.

Being human, people experience traumas, and some are worse than others. As many people out in the world, I experienced bullying. Bullying was my trauma. Being bullied was tough. Bullying was the hardest part of my life, that I had to face alone. Some people think it is a part of life or how it makes kids tough, but it is a mental and physical breakdown of a person. It is a scar that sticks with them forever. It has stuck with me for at least fifteen years of my life, and still counting. Bullying has become more like a virus; it is spreading all over the world. Being singled out for how you look or being slightly different than the world's creative standards.

Are there any purposes of a bully or bullies? Are bullies not all the same? How do you heal and rekindle the light that is within you? I have had these questions in my mind for a while now. No one seems to be sure of what the answers are. So, I wrote my own answers. My own opinions.

Phase one: How the Story Begins

Dear Diary,

I hate it here! I hate my life! Why is it that I am the only person going through hell and back right now? Minding your own business also gets me beat up and talked about. Everyone just laughs at me. No one is here for me, no one likes me… Why am I here? Is it worth it for me?

I have always wanted to become someone else, so I did not have to face the reality of my own life. It was much easier just being alone, no opinions, no questions, and no other unwelcoming company. It is easier to just disappear when you believe that you are the problem. Your mind goes back and forth about everything that is wrong with you. You begin to believe every ugly thing that is said to you, and when you accept the ugliness, you become one with it. And when someone compliments you, you naturally think they are lying. So that is what I did, eliminated the problem.

I was always planning how to escape this world, just as I learned from some of my favorite nineties cartoon characters. They would always seem to run away from their problems. I found the heaviest stick in the yard that I could carry alone, and on the end of that stick was a scarf filled with things I presumed I needed to live off on, my favorite toy, some snacks, and a water bottle. My plan was to leave at night, while everyone was asleep. I was clearly upset and had enough, but instead my grandma stopped me on my way.

She said, umh! Where are you going? I said, grandma would you be sad if I ran away from home. The other kids here are so mean to me and I do not get along with anyone. As she wiped the tears from my eyes, she said; Yes! Why would you do something like that? My head slowly dropped in her soft wrinkled hands, it felt like a relief, a safe place to be.

Grandma's hands were always like pillows! She said something to me that made me change my mind that night. "Well, I love you," she said. "We do care, you are important to us whether they see it now or not. However, you have to know how important you are to yourself." Grandma looked at me and smiled. I cried a long time before I could fall to sleep. She really saved me that night, and plenty of other nights too.

The next few years went by and it was the start of a brand-new school year, I was so excited. I laid out my school clothes the night before. I got up bright and early for school the next day. As usual everyone has on their best first day outfits, in the hallways taking selfies, discussing their long summers, and talking about the new kids in town. I remember exactly what I was wearing that day. I had on black socks with the white forces, and denim blue jeans with a red and white striped shirt.

I had to learn everything all over again, especially how to make new friends. Unfortunately, I was the new kid in town, so I stood out more than ever before.

I was born and raised in the south; I was a young girl just trying to be what everyone wanted me to be. I did not have a clue of what I wanted out of life, I just heard what everyone else wanted for me. As a child I listened to everyone else's needs and wants for me.

I grew up an only child, but I was not alone. I had a best friend; she and I were sisters. We were as close as friends could be, up until the second or third grade. She had moved away, and we had said our goodbyes. I really did not know what to think, maybe she would come back, but time just seemed to move on. I was very saddened by this; it was the first time in my life I felt loneliness. I thought about what I would do without my best friend, or what will happen next. You would just think to make new friends, but it was not that simple. I did not know how to make any friends. That shy awkward person was me. Most of the time I just played alone.

There was a group of kids that lived next door, who I wanted to be friends with, but it just never happened, they were never my friends. These people kept me around as a literal punching bag; they were different from me. I thought if I hung out with them and continued to be nice to them, that maybe they would not hurt me. I was not the only person they treated badly or bullied. I saw it happen many times to others, but I never stood up for them or tried to help them.

I was glad it was not me this time they were picking on. It sounds horrible I know, but back then it was you and no one else, and you dare not to jump in. I had been bullied for the majority of my life. That was the next chapter for me; it was a chapter I expected to go on forever. It honestly felt like forever, I had no control.

When I was about eight years old, I would walk with my head down. Everywhere I went people would tell me; hold your head up, you might walk into something. I did not know how to walk with my head up and when I tried it was awkward. I was a queen without my crown! I could not balance it all.

I had extremely low self-esteem. I was body shamed at an early age, so I did not find myself beautiful. Most of the kids I knew called me ugly and I accepted that. I became uglier with my attitude and how I treated others. I was a powerhouse of anger. I lost faith in everything.

I grew up on Batchelor street, where I thought the world was no bigger than that. Batchelor street was a dead end. It is where most of my feelings and emotions generated itself. Just like that familiar dead end, my emotions had nowhere else to turn.

Pain on Paper

Instead my emotions just got bigger and a lot darker over time.

The bad had outweighed the good when it came to that side of town. I barely go back to visit; I relive every part of my life from that period of time. Most of my memories involve mostly me fighting to defend myself. I did not have any other way to protect myself, I never really wanted to hurt anyone. But fighting back seemed to be my only answer, it was three against one on a dead-end street. It felt as if I did not have another choice.

I felt the punches and the name-calling, the tears rolling down my cheeks, the rage that grew underneath, I felt the pain of a young girl that was trapped by the tricks and antics that still go on in our young people today.

In my mind they were my friends. We went over to each other's house, played games that we should not have played, went to the same church, school, and rode the same bus. They were all I knew. At

school, on the bus and at home, the constant
bullying was swallowing me whole. I spent most of
my time alone, I did not want people around me and
I focused on how others perceived me everywhere I
went. This was my normal day to day!

My neighborhood was a very, very
overwhelming place to be. I did not view it as
home. There were too many things going on with
me that my parents or teachers did not know about.
It was not a safe place. As soon as you told an adult
about someone bothering you the whole school
would know about it, in the matter of seconds.
Teachers did not do much back then either. Nine
times out of ten, they forget about the situation. Our
world was not on the top of the list at the time. It is
taught that when we are just kids; we will get over
it. I guess that could have been the mindset of some
people. I was afraid that the bullying would get
worse over time. I never spoke about it out loud
with anyone. There were many days when I would

come home in tears off the bus because of all the mean and hurtful things kids would say to me. My mother told me; if I came home another day crying, she was going to cut my behind herself. It was her way of telling me not to be anyone's punching bag. I know it hurt her to see her only child in pain and she could not do anything about it. We were just kids but that does not make it any less serious. I believe what my mother said gave me the push I needed because I was not about to get a beat down from a bunch of bullies and then come home to another beat down from my mother. That was not happening.

After a few days, while getting off the bus one of my bullies stuck his finger in his mouth and stuffed it down my ear. It was so disgusting, and I was so angry. I wanted to fight back; I really did. I wanted to hurt others the way they were hurting me. All I could see was red. I screamed and fought back as hard as I could but once again, they just laughed at me.

Many times, after that if one person bothered me another attacker would push or hit me in the back. I had to be forced to defend myself because I had no one else, no brothers or sisters that could protect me. I had to fight, even when I was too tired or afraid to do so. I had to fight so maybe they would leave me alone, but it was like they enjoyed fighting. It just encouraged them even more. My pain was humorous to them, it was all for their enjoyment.

I remember so well, when we were in the backyard of my bullies, playing on the swings. All of a sudden, my bully decided to punch me in the stomach, repeatedly. As the tears fell, a great deal of fear arose. My bullies had become more and more physical by the day. They threw dirt in my eyes, jumped me in my own yard and always callcd me names other than my own. Almost every day I had to fight physically and mentally.

Pain on Paper

Looking back, I can see the lasting affects bullying has had on my life. Believing that I was everything they said I was. They had full control over my life and there was no escaping it. I was bigger than the other kids my age so they would call me fat and pull my hair. I wanted to fit in with them, I wanted to be their friend so badly, it didn't matter to me how they treated me because after a while I just thought I was always going to be stuck where I was, I didn't see a way out. I had lost all hope of ever being accepted for being me. I lost my self-respect; I had started looking for attention in men.

Men gave me the attention that felt good, smelled good, sounded good and looked so good. Of course, they were much older than me, but I did not care. Once I figured out what a man liked or what he wanted, I played off their feelings and emotions. Given them all false hope of what they never received. Telling them things they liked to hear. I even started wearing tight clothes to show off my body, I had no clue what I was inviting in. They would tell me how sexy they thought I was and how they wanted to be my man. They gave me money and bought me things from the little convenience store that sat on the end of the street. I liked the attention so much I started lying about my age, some guys did not care how old I was. "Age is just a number, baby!" That was their favorite line.

Also, because I was born with six fingers; a lot of the kids did not want to talk to me. The kids did not want me to touch them during group activities. I would get questions like "Are you some kind of alien or something?" because it was something different, they have not seen before, they choose to be mean or afraid of me. This gave me the feeling of not belonging in the world.

The name calling continued on for a few years, but my own mental destruction went on into my adult years. Our minds are powerful, I held on to everything that was said or done to me. Never forgive anyone for anything. Just held it all in, like a dripping sponge. I could have exploded with the amount of anger I had. I wreaked of it, I learned how to mask it all, I learned how to put it away like my anger was a tangible object I could place on the shelf.

The smile I wore, it was fake! I wore it so much that I started to believe it myself. I made people think everything was okay when I was truly broken inside. Worried all the time about how a person saw me. I was never free to be who I was supposed to be.

After everything is said, you start to really ask yourself, "Are these things really true about me"? I started to hate myself, for being different, for not looking how everyone else wanted me to look. I wanted to run away, I thought of ways to end my life because of bullying. I was extremely exhausted, trying to be a person everyone would rather have in their lives or not. I knew that my bullies had a dislike for me that even if I was to be just my true self it was not good enough for them. Mentally, I thought of myself not being good enough for anyone. Not even my parents.

I felt that I had failed my own parents because I was not all that I could be. I overcompensated by always being respectful to my elders, receiving straight A's, and being more of an adult than I had to be. I had no choice but to become a bookworm, math was my favorite subject. That is how I became stuck or obsessed in this perfect box. I wanted to please everyone, pretending I was so perfect, doing everything they way it should be done.

I did not understand why God had created me, I believed I was useless in the world. Maybe with no purpose at all. I wondered why I deserved to live. I was at my lowest point. I remember being on the bathroom floor, sobbing, praying to God that He sends me a husband, a best friend at the age of nine.

He could be my best friend for the rest of my life. Someone real that I could share something with. Someone who loves me like no other. I needed that in my life. Even as an adult. I was still searching for acceptance. Needing to be loved, I want to be needed and heard. I could not hardly bare the feeling of being alone anymore. I did not want to.

Wow! I was really a child trying to decide if I should take my own life and praying for a husband. I do not believe at the time I really understood what I was praying for, I just knew I needed some help. I was a bit desperate and at that moment my heart turned to God. He was the only person left to ask. It is amazing how people do not realize it sometimes, but as children we could be at our lowest point in life. We carry so much inside, we often feel as though it is our fault, that we brought this on ourselves somehow.

Often, I would listen to music and sing along at the top of my lungs. Music just made sense! I could see myself in almost any song I sang. I felt like I was not living the life I was living. Music made me feel in love, impowered, beautiful and made me feel like I was not the only person in the world going through things. Music made me want so much more out of life.

I found myself drawing and keeping a diary but as I grew older, I put those things away, including music. I started to forget about my writings. I just buried my head in the sand. More so like a robot. I turned my emotions completely off from the world.

Phase Two: Morphed

Yes, I was the new girl in town. Just like anyone I was a bit nervous about starting a new school. I felt different about this school, only because I knew I could create a different me. Being at a new school allowed me to be the person I thought I wanted to become. It was a fresh start; I had a second chance.

I made new friends, which built up this newfound confidence in me. I felt like I was starting life again. The bullies were gone, and I never had to see them again.

But before we move on! You need to be sure you understand that there is so much more to bullying than just words or what you allow people to say to you, it can also become physical. There is so much more to bullying than we may ever know, and people have been creative with the idea of bullying. More creative in ways to bully other people, mostly our young people.

No one supports the hurt of others but do not allow anyone to hurt you for the pleasure of them. Find help and let someone know about what is going on with you. There is a huge difference between just fighting and defending yourself. If you feel threatened by anyone, you do have every right to defend yourself. Never be afraid to stand up for yourself or someone else in need. You never know, you might be saving that person's life. You might even change how they view the world.

Bullying gave people this power that they thought they had over others, it instilled a great deal of fear and anxiety. Physically getting punched in the stomach repeatedly was painful. I was terrified to stand up for myself, most of the time I would just run home crying. But there came a time where I had to defend myself.

Foolishly, I still became friends with the same people who would beat me and throw dirt in my eyes. I thought truly this was a sign of manipulation because the only time bullies were ever nice to me was to use my toys during Christmas time.

Bullying for me did not just end in my neighborhood or in school but continued in my home. In some cases, even our parents can be bullies. We may not have the understanding to separate something meant to be harmful or funny when you have been going through a lot of hurt.

Pain on Paper

Parents may not realize the weight of their words until it is too late; some never realize it at all. With my parents, it was a different kind of bully. This bully used words like I "can't" do something such as cheerleading because I am too fat. At my young age I had associated what my parents said to what the kids were already saying about me. My parents and the other children all were in the same boat together in my mind. Their words hurt me. I held on to those words. I could never forget it. The day came for me to try out for cheerleading, and those words rushed back to the forefront of my mind. I just walked away, never thinking about cheerleading again. I have always wanted to become a cheerleader but because I thought I did not fit the mold or was not what someone else wanted or thought a cheerleader should be, I never became one. I do not place the blame on my parents, but on myself. I take responsibility for what I allowed to move into my mind permanently and stopped me from doing the thing I wanted to do.

I allowed other's words to influence me or my decisions. I never became a cheerleader; the words of others stuck with me and became engraved in my mind. I could not erase them, I could not unhear them. The damage was already done. Yes, I was the new girl in town. Just like anyone I was a bit nervous about starting a new school. I felt different about this school, only because I knew I could create a different me.

Being at a new school allowed me to be the person I thought I wanted to become. It was a fresh start, I had a chance to make new friends, which built up this newfound confidence in me. I felt like I was given a second chance at life. The bullies were gone, and I never had to see them again.

A few months have passed and there is a new girl in town, just as I was. Right away I realized that she was different in a lot of ways I was also. A short time went by and I could see how people began to talk about her and laugh at her. It reminded me so much of how others treated me. They bullied her for the same reason I was bullied, different, we just did not do what everyone else did. Embarrassed I admit, I did the same. I talked about her and laughed at her with the others. I called her names and I even went as far as putting my own hands on her. I just became a bully myself. I did not realize it then, but I had morphed into something I was ashamed of. By the time I knew It, I had already caused much damage in people's lives.

The people I hung around made it feel as though it was okay to be a bully. I had developed a bully mindset. And during that time, I was okay with that. I felt power when I bullied and had others on my side or people that agreed with me. I enjoy others' pain. I forgot what it was like to be bullied, I had become selfish.

Like I said, I had a bully mind set. I knew I had to change, and it was not easy. I had gotten used to

being around people that like me for my bullying
lifestyle for so long that It was hard to get away
from them. Especially because they were around me
all the time it had made it easier for me to fall back
into old habits. I wanted change but also I was
afraid to just be myself, I was worried that if they
noticed I wanted to be different, and that I didn't
want to be mean to the girl who sat in front of me in
class every other day, that they would turn on me. I
was not so sure if I could handle that again.

Some people may say it had a lot to do with peer
pressure, but honestly, I had a choice and I made it.
I made the decision I wanted to be on the "other
side" for once, instead of being bullied again. I did
not even think twice about the girl's feelings, or
what I could have put her through physically. Just
like that I became what I was afraid of most. I did
not even realize what I had done or become. I
wanted others to feel how I felt, alone, and unheard.
I did not know I had a sick way of thinking. I

should have stood up for those who could not stand up for themselves. I realized how wrong I was. I apologize to anyone that I may have hurt, though I was young and hurting, I should have never treated a person like the way I was treated. I honestly should have known better.

Phase Three: Morally Contaminated

By now a few more years have passed, I have graduated Ridge View High School and I find myself attending Francis Marion University. My childhood haunted me after high school, right into college. It really caught me off guard that even when we transition into something new, your past keeps tagging along with you.

I realized you cannot run from your past; it follows you until you address the situation or the root of your issues. Repeatedly, I have been as nice as I believe I could be to people. I have been the kind and loving spirit that people would take advantage of. I think for the most part, I allowed myself to be used more because I did not want to be looked at as mean or boring. It was my first year of college, I wanted to explore and have a great time. I wanted a group of friends, a family that I could hang out with and do everything together. I wanted to bond together and become sisters. I was hung up on things I have seen on social media, groups of friends all taking selfies together. I thought that could be my life.

I thought to join a sorority, but yet again I was not like them, I could not relate to them and when I say "them" I mean people in my age group, my roommates in college. They could not understand me. The young ladies did not try to get to know me, they acted on their own emotions and self-made opinions about me. Several ladies had a meeting about why they did not like me, while wanting me to sit and listen to all their reasons of why. I held on to that pain for a long time. It was cruel and malicious of them but in the back of my mind I wanted to curse each one of them out. But I just sat there and smiled, I let them have their moment because it was not worth my time or effort.

After that meeting I simply got up and just left the room. I cried for hours! I felt like I had done something wrong. Maybe I just tried too hard to be their friend, in any effort I never meant to push myself on anyone. I blamed myself for what happened that night and it left me bitter for a while. I knew most of those girls before college, I thought they were nice to everyone, but I guess I prejudged too quickly and that is on me. I could never look at them the same again. However, I do forgive them, I can honestly say I do not hold anything against them. These young ladies were trying to figure themselves out just as I was. And I love my freedom, so I choose to forgive.

It is funny how we can base our lives off the

things we view on social media. I wanted to be just like the girls or people I had seen on Facebook or Instagram. At some point I found myself idolizing or glorifying the ones on these social media accounts. I wanted my life to model what they had or if the person looked a certain way, I wanted to look that way also; just to be liked by others or to be better than the others around me. Who have you wanted to be like or idolized? Was this person on social media or maybe this person was around you? Either way being your authentic self is better than any person or persons you can compare yourself to anywhere. I did not understand this at that time, I lacked the courage to be me. I did not have to try to be someone else because it did not work out anyway.

God wanted me to be more of me, when I tried to be something I was not, more of me would show up. Most things that I wanted to do did not line up with God so in efforts to rebel against Him, I would force myself to fit in with many different other things, unpleasing. However, he would somehow show me myself. I would then not want to participate in those things everyone else wanted me to do, the feeling was so strong, I could not help but turn away from other temptations that were not in his agreement with my life. It is like I am in a force field. Imagine you are standing in the middle of it, if you go more in one direction than the other, the farther you go, the more force or pull you feel behind you to center you back to the middle. A place of balance. A place of peace. For some of us that is a hard place to be in. We fight with our flesh more and more each day because it is something else, we would rather be doing.

I knew being a bully was not who I was, so I thought maybe if I showed people how nice I am they will love me, right? Only if I knew how misguided I was then, could I have corrected myself on the nonsense going on in my head. I allowed people to single me out and place unnecessary hurt in my heart.

People who wanted to love me, I doubted them. I thought they were just trying to hurt me like everyone else, so I built up all these walls around myself. No one could get in or close enough to me, not even my family. I became very insecure while in college, I was afraid of putting myself out there or to play any sports. Always in my room. I am always second guessing myself and the things I should be doing or should have done in life. I wanted to be left alone, I want to stop thinking so much about how others may or may not feel about me. I realized I had to change if I wanted my life or situations to change. During college God got me alone, there were times when I could hear and learn his voice. It took my obedience for me to trust in God, but he showed up every time. He showed up even when I was wrong, He heard me when no one else did, I was never alone.

Pain on Paper

Phase Four: Matthew 6:14-15

"For if you forgive [a]others their trespasses [their reckless and willful sins], your heavenly Father will also forgive you. But if you do not forgive others [nurturing your hurt and anger with the result that it interferes with your relationship with God], then your Father will not forgive your trespasses."

(Matthew 6:14-15, Amplified Bible)

We all have something to be forgiven for. I will always choose to forgive the ones who have hurt me. Trust me, it is not always an easy thing to do. My bullies had a job to do, to bring greatness out of Me; purpose that themselves could not have understood. I have learned to embrace my bullies. They allowed me to work harder and pushed me to extraordinary limits. If it were not for my bullies, I would not have recognized my potential, because some bullies come after what intimidates or threatens them the most. I expect many more bullies to come to try and distract me along my journey; a learning journey that will bring about new and exciting challenges, that I can be proud of.

Bullies all have something in common, like me it could be past hurts and emotions. One thing I noticed about my bullies along the way is that they did not have both parents in the same household together, I know that could not have been easy for them. It would not have been easy for me. I was very fortunate to have both my parents in the same household, and I'm not taking up for the person or persons that may have hurt you or us in the past but if you are a person like me, I would hope you find a way to better process your pain instead of into other people. I have learned that is a vicious cycle and it is not the best way to go. In hopes of forgiveness, I never meant to hurt the people around me. I could not handle my pain very well, and I had no healthy source of an outlet at the time. Yet, there are no amount of excuses that I could give anyone for my actions or choice of words. I take full responsibility for anyone I may have damaged or who I may have caused any type of pain, for that I do apologize.

All in all, I have chosen to forgive myself. It is an important step that you cannot skip. In order to move on in a positive way, you must forgive yourself. I forgive myself for the hurt that I caused and for not knowing myself sooner. Not knowing the value of my life and the purpose of my life brings to others around me. I forgive myself for not allowing people to love me, for not loving myself. I forgive myself for thinking less than what I ever deserved. I hope that you will have the power to forgive yourself. I do not want you to go on in life reliving the mistakes you have made. You made the mistake, do not let the mistake make you. Learn from it, allow it to better you and move on into your future. Remember to not look back into a door you decide to close, it is a part of forgiveness.

Pain on Paper

Phase Five: Socially Compatible

In my opinion, children have it the hardest when growing up into a world with a lot of suggestions of who, and what they should be. They do not just receive expectations from parents but from peers too. We do not give children enough time to imagine and to be creative, to be free because we all want the best for our children, but the best has already been done. I felt as if I were placed into the box that everyone or most people wanted me to fit in and I was trying really hard to fit into that box. I wanted to be in that mold because I wanted everyone to be proud of me, I wanted everyone to like me. I wanted to please others even if it meant for me to be unhappy. Sometimes even now, I still find myself trying to be the best at everything others want me to be the best at, instead of being the best for myself. I am afraid of disappointing the people close to me. I dread the phrase "no, I'm not mad but

I'm disappointed in you". It is because I was into what society said was correct or the natural way to go. The natural expectations of life.

In my experience, growing into an adult has been difficult, trying to get past the anxiety of disappointing others but trying not to disappoint myself. Other people's disappointments became my own. I know I lost plenty of opportunities because I worry so much about the wrong things, so much on the wrong people. Learn from me, it is not worth your time or effort for you to be concerned about what others say, how they view you. People will judge but it all depends on how you are equipped to handle it.

Oh, my goodness! I could have been so much further along than this, not only for me but for my family, and for the people who need to hear my voice. My mind was so caught up in the wrong things. Now I am paying for it, and it is much harder to get where I am going now versus if I had gotten what I needed then. So, learn from me, if you are being bullied or the pressure of life is weighing you down, just remember that you are worth it. You are worth going through the fight, you are worth more than any struggle you could be going through. Your pain and losses will not be in vain, but for your victory, to say you made it!

Phase Six: Means of Release

As children, it is easy to get into our heads because we soak up everything, but do not always say what is going on. Maybe because we will not think an adult can help us nor understand. I would not go to my parents or teachers about how or what was going on with me because I was too afraid it would not make a difference. I did not think that they could protect me, especially because they were not around all the time. I could not stand to be attacked any more than I already was. It just seemed like my parents could not tell what was happening right under their noses, and I do not blame them.

My parents were hard-working, and I was incredibly grateful for them. Plus, most of the time they would not have known unless I told them what was really happening with me. All these years I kept to myself, bottled up, not wanting to open up about how bullying has affected my life. I withdrew from society because I did not believe they understood.

In college, I was alone a lot. I chose to make the decision to speak to God. I wanted to make that choice on my own. I started praying more often, almost every night. I prayed that I would find out who I am to God. I was struggling with who I was for such a long time and I needed some guidance. God, answered. I did not realize that it was Him. I started waking up feeling very refreshed. Each day I would walk around to our shared bathroom and I would start staring at myself. That went on for quite a while. I would not only stare at myself but I acknowledged how beautiful I was, and it felt good. I mentally just thought I was such a beautiful person. I even told random people around me how beautiful they were.

I wanted to continue to feel good, so I started making small changes in my life. I continued to pray and started going to church. I was attending Francis Marion University, in Florence county, but I drove home every weekend. I committed my Sundays to Christ.

Mt. Moriah Baptist church is my home church. Being in church made me feel closer to Christ. If you grew up in a Baptist church, you know after service they would ask anyone to come up for prayer or to become a member. Sometimes they would ask if you would like to be baptized. Well, Mt. Moriah did such things at the end of every service. At the end of service, when the question was asked "Did anyone want to become a member or to be baptized", I would feel this unbearable pull on my heart. I felt like God was calling me to be baptized. I was trying my best to avoid it, but it was constantly on my mind, then one Sunday I said, "Okay God, Let's do this", I got up and went to the front of the whole church. I asked to be baptized. I was truly terrified! I did not understand what was going to happen next, but once I was baptize things started happening.

I started meeting people who became an important part of my life. Habits that I thought I could never break, I just stopped, never thinking about them again. Of course, there was some time in between each event but everything was relativity quick.

In the course of two years, there were times when I did not think I could live up to the person God wanted me to be, I had to encourage myself to move. I told myself plenty of times, "Arica, you can and will succeed in life and in your purpose. Just get there, you are one more step closer." Sure, those negative thoughts come back fast but replacing those same thoughts with something positive. Be intentional! You feel fear rising up, be quick! Say, no not to today fear, I am on my way to see purpose. Shut those negative thought down. They are powerless unless you give them power.

The people around me pushed me to do better, to become a better me. They prayed over me and interceded for me. They taught me life skills that I could actually apply to my life and see real life changing results.

Short time after, I was reminded of my writings as a child, but I really was not receiving it. I did not see writing anywhere in my near future. I even prayed against it, asking the Lord is there something else I can do instead. But I guess not, so I started writing.

Surprised, writing has become therapy for me, a way out of my own head. There is no one to judge me, and the best part is if you mess up, you can rip the paper into a million different pieces just to start over again. It is just penning to paper, and no one has power over what you will release but you.

I will be honest with you; it has taken some time to fall in love with writing. I had to practice. It has been rough. I had to sit down, open my heart and open files that I kept closed for a long time; files I did not attend to ever open. I had to be transparent with me first. Asking myself, do I really want to go down that rabbit hole? Never realized I had so much to say. I even hated the things I had to write but the relief I felt afterward made me feel free. I cried plenty of times while writing, just pouring my hurt on to paper.

There were times I had to walk away from it, because I did not want to reread what I was writing. Often, I felt like I was reading someone else's story and not my own. Once I reread for the hundredth time, it became easier. It became beautiful even with the scars. I will always remember my past, the pain I went through, but I realized writing it down, reading it to myself became beautiful, because it was healing to my soul.

I have found that having an outlet keeps you from having things bottled up inside, keeps your heart and intentions pure. When there is no one around that can help you, write it down, find a way to help yourself until you build the confidence you need to share your story with someone. Your outlet can be anything you want it to be. Some people workout, some just like to read, paint, or even make music. Whatever it might be, just be sure it is right for you.

Phase Seven: Completeness

Did you know I would shut down in the middle of the day and cry? As you now know I practice self-harm. I was angry with God for placing me in this world. If I did not have approval from the world I would just fall apart. And dwell on everything so imperfect about myself.

I had lost myself, and after all these years I am putting myself back together, with you, every day. I am regaining my strength to win and to conquer every task placed in front of me. I am much bolder than I was just a few years ago. Much happier because I have decided to live for myself. Living for my purpose.

I have decided to allow someone to love me. I did not know the true meaning of love and someone being there for me until I met my husband. Before I received the attention that was only for a blink of an eye… something quick like a fix. I did not know this then, but I realize now that God was saving the perfect man for me.

I am taking my life back and no one or situation has power over me or how my life should be. It took me a while to start trusting in God again. But he has shown me love beyond my imagination. Time and time again I ran in the opposite direction because I was scared of everything I could be. I was afraid to tap into something I have never experienced before. However, I cannot run away anymore. It is time to face what I have been avoiding, and that is everything within me that I have to offer to the world. I need to leave behind something more valuable than just being a wife, mom, and a daughter. I need to leave a footprint that are words of healing to people of all walks of life, God's people. Healing in a positive and steady way each day.

Look at your life as being a masterpiece. I see my life as being a recipe. Some of us just need the right ingredients added to our lives, to come out with something delicious on the other side. You would not want to place the rotten or expired things in it because it would not be a pleasant taste. Guess what I'm trying to say is that sometimes we can be in a place where we have not forgiven those who have hurt us in the past, so we continue to hold on to these rotten things adding them into our lives as we go. When we are hurt, we often deflect our pain into others, without meaning to. However, when we make a choice to forgive, we make the choice to become that delicious something on the other side. We make a choice to become free, and in that freedom there so much power.

No matter the size of the situation, you will make it through. Trust me it will not all happen overnight, but you will make it a step at a time. Start with making a choice; a choice to become a better you. Physically our bodies heal, that is the easy part. Healing your mind really takes effort and may take a few years for some people. As humans we never really forget what we have been through in the past, especially if it was damaging enough to leave a scar in your memory. However, we can heal our minds.

Bullying left a scar in my mind but does not hurt anymore. Now it is a symbol of my victory because

Pain on Paper

I made it through. Bullying has no shape, color, or size. Bullying can be used or done anywhere; social media is a perfect tool. Social media bullying still hurts and probably worse, because it reaches so many more people with the same agenda. It is funny how people can be a lot less fearless when it comes to a bully on social media, behind a screen. Bullies are going through something too.

We cannot allow anyone to stop our healing process, or to dim our light anymore. We must take a stand for ourselves and become whole. I am learning to love who I am, my flaws and all. Everything that I thought was imperfect about me is perfect. No one else can be me, no one can be you. I cannot be you because God said I only need one of you. When God created you, He did not create you without purpose, you were never a mistake. I have purpose and I do deserve much more in life, than beating myself up about things I cannot change.

Pain on Paper

Learn to encourage yourself each day. Keep telling yourself you can, you will be whole and that your past does not define you. Believe in yourself and trust the process. We all have a voice to be heard, and it is time that someone has heard it!

As an adult my healing process is simple. I learned how to write every emotion on paper. It is my pain on paper. Though I call it "Pain on Paper", I really do write down all of my emotions. Happy or sad, it is how I learned to become comfortable with my own writing. It is also how I organize my thought process.

When I write all my hurts transform into something else amazing. Writing gives me a fresh start, a reboot, and a chance to self-reflect. Writing made a way for me to forgive my past, so that I may have a future to live. It gave me freedom to express how I truly feel about things. Writing did not just become my outlet or a way out, but it became my friend. Writing listened to the words I had to say, writing was the key to my caged mind. I know this may not be for everyone but just take the time to sit down for yourself.

Think about everything that may have stopped you from being the best person you could be, the obstacle in life that you were afraid of. Write them all out and make goals for yourself that you will become the best you that you can possibly be from here on out. Explain those obstacles and emotions to yourself and then encourage yourself, all on paper. Invest that time and energy into you. Solve what makes you tick! So that maybe you can gain power and control back over your life.

It is through my writing that I learned how afraid I was of what people around me had to say or thought about me. My past of being bullied had me trapped in a place of unforgiveness. I thought everyone around me was talking negatively about me. I wanted to stay in what was comfortable for me, going around day to day, in my mess. I did not want to move out my own way to grow or to conquer the feelings that came along with being hurt or emotionally damaged. I created a goal for myself that I was going to learn who I was, by taking the mental walls down one by one. Learning how to be the person God wants me to be. Listening for His voice and following Him all the way. It will take some time but If you are willing to go through the process you will make it, it will be worth in the end.

This is my story, I wanted to share with you. I wanted to share my story because I know I am not the only one who has had a hard time with bullying or in my case also becoming a bully. Understand that you are not alone and there are others like us who have been bullied, abused in many ways, or just may be feeling the pressure of the world on their shoulders. Do not feel as if you have to keep any of your hurts to yourself, speak out and do not worry about the naysayers. Allow this to be your start of a brand-new journey, do not delay your healing process any longer than you already have. This is about you, so let us get to where we are supposed to be, our purpose. Living, breathing, and walking all in our own unique purpose.

Here is my challenge to you! Write your pain on paper, allow your hurt to go into the world to manifest into something beautiful. Write your story and allow your voice to be heard. It may be the very next thing someone needs to hear from you.

Pain on Paper

Journal Entry One:

Pain on Paper

Journal Entry Two:

Pain on Paper

Journal Entry Three:

Pain on Paper

Journal Entry Four:

Pain on Paper

Journal Entry Five:

Pain on Paper

Contact Information

Email Address: Arica.Robinson99@outlook.com

Facebook: Arica Robinson

Pain on Paper

www.ingramcontent.com/pod-product-compliance
Lightning Source LLC
Chambersburg PA
CBHW060354050426
42449CB00011B/2990